The Man in the Bowler Hat

A Terribly Exciting Affair

by A. A. Milne

A SAMUEL FRENCH ACTING EDITION

SAMUEL FRENCH

FOUNDED 1830

New York Hollywood London Toronto

SAMUELFRENCH.COM

THE MAN IN THE BOWLER HAT

CHARACTERS

JOHN
MARY
HERO
HEROINE
CHIEF VILLAIN
BAD MAN

The Man In The Bowler Hat

The Scene is MARY'S *sitting room—the most ordinary sitting room in the world.* JOHN *and* MARY, *two of the most ordinary people, he in the early forties, she in the late thirties, are sitting in front of the fire after dinner. He, as usual, is reading the paper; she, as usual, is knitting. They talk in a desultory way.*

MARY. Did I tell you that Mrs. Patchett has just had another baby?

JOHN. *(Not looking up from his paper)* Yes, dear, you told me.

MARY. Did I? Are you sure?

JOHN. Last week.

MARY. But she only had it yesterday. Mr. Patchett told me this morning when I was ordering the cauliflower.

JOHN. Ah! Then perhaps you told me she was going to have one.

MARY. Yes, I think that must have been it.

JOHN. This is the one that she was going to have?

MARY. It weighed seven pounds exactly.

JOHN. Of course, being a grocer, he would have the scales ready. Boy or girl?

MARY. Boy.

JOHN. The first boy, isn't it?

MARY. The second.

JOHN. *(Sticking to it)* The first one that weighed seven pounds exactly.

(They are silent again—he reading, she knitting.)

MARY. Anything in the paper tonight?

JOHN. *(Turning over the paper)* A threatened strike of boiler-makers.

MARY. Does that matter very much?

JOHN. It says here that the situation is extremely serious.

MARY. Tell me about it.

JOHN. *(Not very good at it)* Well, the—er—boiler-makers are threatening to strike. *(Weightily)* They are threatening not to make any more—er—boilers.

MARY. Kitchen boilers?

JOHN. *(With an explanatory gesture)* Boilers. They are threatening not to make any more of them. And—well—that's how it is. *(Returning to his paper)* The situation is extremely serious. Exciting scenes have been witnessed.

MARY. What sort of scenes?

JOHN. Well, naturally, when you have a lot of men threatening not to make any more boilers . . . and—er—a lot of other men threatening that if they *don't* make any—well, exciting scenes are witnessed. *Have* been witnessed by this man, this special correspondent.

MARY. *(After a pause)* It's a funny thing that nothing exciting ever happens to *us*.

JOHN. It depends what you mean by exciting. I went round in 95 last Saturday—as I think I told you.

MARY. Yes, but I mean something really thrilling—and dangerous. Like a novel—or on the stage.

JOHN. My dear Mary, nothing like that ever happens in real life. I mean it wouldn't happen to *us*.

MARY. Would you like it if it did?

(He says nothing for a moment. Then he puts down his paper, and sits there, thinking. At last he turns to her.)

JOHN. *(Almost shyly)* I used to imagine things like

6

that happening. Years ago. Rescuing a beautiful maiden and—and all that sort of thing. And being wrecked on a desert island with her. . . . *(He turns away from her, staring into his dreams)* Or pushing open a little green door in a long high wall, and finding myself in a wonderful garden under the bluest of blue skies, and waiting, waiting . . . for something. . . .

MARY. I used to imagine things too. People fighting duels because of me. . . . Silly, isn't it? Nothing ever really happens like that.

JOHN. *(Still with his thoughts)* No. . . .

(At this moment a STRANGE MAN comes in. Contrary to all etiquette, he is wearing a Bowler Hat and an overcoat, and has a half-smoked cigar in his mouth. He walks quickly across the room and sits down in a chair with his back to the audience. JOHN and MARY, deep in their thoughts, do not notice him.)

MARY. *(Looking into the fire)* I suppose we're too old for it now.

JOHN. I suppose so.

MARY. If it had only happened once—just for the memories.

JOHN. So that we could say to each other— Good lord! what's that?

(It was the crack of a revolver. No mistaking it, even by JOHN, who has never been much of a hand with revolvers.)

MARY. *(Frightened)* John!

(There is a scuffling noise outside the door. They look eagerly towards it. Then suddenly there is dead silence. The MAN IN THE BOWLER HAT flicks some of his cigar ash onto the carpet—MARY'S carpet.)

JOHN. Look!

(Very slowly the door begins to open. Through the

7

crack comes a long, sinuous hand. The door opens farther, and the hand is followed by a long, sinuous body. Still the MAN IN THE BOWLER HAT *says nothing. Then the door is closed, and leaning up against it, breathing rather quickly, is the* HERO, *in his hand a revolver.* JOHN *and* MARY *look at each other wonderingly.)*

JOHN. *(With a preliminary cough)* I—I beg your pardon?
HERO. *(Turning quickly, finger to his lips)* H'sh!
JOHN. *(Apologetically)* I beg your pardon!

(The HERO *listens anxiously at the door. Then, evidently reassured for the moment he comes towards them.)*

HERO. *(To* JOHN*)* Quick, take this! *(He presses his revolver into* JOHN's *hand.)*
JOHN. I—er—what do I—
HERO. *(To* MARY*)* And you! This! *(He takes another revolver from his hip pocket and presses it into* MARY's *hand.)*
MARY. Thank you. Do we—
HERO. *(Sternly)* H'sh!
MARY. Oh, I beg your pardon.
HERO. Listen!

(They ALL *listen.* JOHN *and* MARY *have never listened so intently before, but to no purpose. They hear nothing.)*

JOHN. *(In a whisper)* What is it?
HERO. Nothing.
JOHN. Yes, that's what *I* heard.
HERO. Have you got a— *(He breaks off and broods.)*
MARY. A what?
HERO. *(Shaking his head)* No, it's too late now.
JOHN. *(To* MARY*)* Haven't we got one?
MARY. I ordered one on Saturday, but it **hasn't** come.

8

HERO. You wait here—that will be best. I shall be back in a moment.

JOHN. What do we do?

HERO. Listen. That's all. Listen.

JOHN. *(Eagerly)* Yes, yes.

HERO. I shall be back directly.

(Just as he is making for the window, the door opens and the HEROINE—*obviously—comes in. They stand gazing at each other.)*

HEROINE. Oh! *(But with a world of expression in it.)*

HERO. Oh! *(With even more expression.)*

HEROINE. My love!

HERO. My beautiful!

(They meet and are locked in an embrace.)

JOHN. *(To* MARY*)* I suppose they're engaged to be married.

MARY. Oh, I think they must be.

JOHN. They've evidently *met* before.

HERO. *(Lifting his head for a moment)* My Dolores! *(He bites her neck again.)*

JOHN. *(To* MARY*)* I think this must be both "How do you do" *and* "Goodbye."

MARY. *(Wistfully)* He is very good-looking.

JOHN. *(Casually)* Oh, do you think so? Now *she's* pretty, if you like.

MARY. *(Doubtfully)* Ye-es. Very bad style, of course.

JOHN. *(Indignantly)* My dear Mary—

HEROINE. *(To* HERO*)* Quick, quick, you must go!

HERO. Never—now that I have found you again.

HEROINE. Yes, yes! My father is hot upon your tracks. He will be here at any moment in his two-seater.

HERO. *(Turning pale)* Your father!

HEROINE. I walked on ahead to warn you. He has come for—IT!

JOHN. *(To* MARY*)* What on earth's IT?
HERO. *(Staggering)* IT!
HEROINE. Yes.
JOHN. *(To* MARY*)* Income-tax collector.
HERO. The Rajah's Ruby!
MARY. Oh, how exciting!
HEROINE. Yes, he knows you have it. He is determined to wrest it from you.
HERO. Never!
JOHN. Well done! Bravo! *(Offering his cigarette case)* Would you care for a— *(But the* HERO *spurns it.)*
HEROINE. There is no mischief he might not do, if once it were in his possession. Three prominent members of Society would be ruined, there would be another war in Mexico and the exchange value of the rouble would be seriously impaired. Promise me you will never give it up.
HERO. I promise.
HEROINE. I must go. I am betraying my father by coming here, but I love you.
JOHN. *(To* MARY*)* She does love him. I thought she did.
MARY. How could she help it?
HERO. I adore you!
JOHN. You see, he adores her too. It certainly looked like it.
MARY. I still don't think she's very good style.
HEROINE. Then—goodbye!

(They embrace again.)

JOHN. *(After a decent interval)* Excuse me, sir, but if you have a train to catch—I mean if your future father-in-law's two-seater is any good at all, oughtn't you to be—er—
HERO. *(Releasing* HEROINE*)* Goodbye! *(He conducts her to the door, gives her a last long lingering look, and lets her go.)*
MARY. *(To herself)* Pretty, of course, in a kind of way, but I must say I don't *like* that style.

(The HERO comes out of his reverie and proceeds to business.)

HERO. *(Briskly to JOHN)* You have those revolvers?

JOHN. Yes.

HERO. Then wait here, and listen. More than one life depends upon it.

JOHN. How many more?

HERO. If you hear the slightest noise—

JOHN. *(Eagerly)* Yes!

HERO. H'sh!

(He goes to the window, waits there listening for a moment, and then slips out. . . . JOHN and MARY remain, their ears outstretched.)

JOHN. *(With a start)* H'sh! What's that?

MARY. What was it, dear?

JOHN. I don't know.

MARY. It's so awkward when you don't quite know what you're listening *for*.

JOHN. H'sh! We were told to listen and we must listen. More than one life depends on it.

MARY. All right, dear.

(They continue to listen. A little weary of it, MARY looks down the barrel of the revolver to see if she can see anything interesting.)

JOHN. *(Observing her)* Don't do that! It's very dangerous to point a loaded revolver at yourself. If anything happened, it would be too late to say afterwards that you didn't mean it.

MARY. Very well, John— Oh, look!

(Again the door opens quickly, and a sinister gentleman in a fur coat inserts himself into the room. We recognize him at once as the CHIEF VILLAIN. Very noiselessly, his back to JOHN and MARY, he creeps along the wall towards the window.)

JOHN. *(In a whisper)* Father-in-law.

11

MARY. Do we— *(She indicates the revolver.)*

JOHN. *(Doubtfully)* I—I suppose— *(He raises his gun hesitatingly.)*

MARY. Oughtn't you to say something first?

JOHN. Yes—er— *(He clears his throat warningly)* Ahem! *(The CHIEF VILLAIN continues to creep towards the window)* You, sir!

MARY. *(Politely)* Do you want anything, or—or anything?

(The CHIEF VILLAIN is now at the window.)

JOHN. Just a moment, sir.

(The CHIEF VILLAIN opens the window and steps out between the curtains.)

MARY. Oh, he's gone!

JOHN. I call that very bad manners.

MARY. Do you think he'll come back?

JOHN. *(With determination)* I shall shoot him like a dog if he does. *(Waiving aside all protests)* Like a dog.

MARY. Yes, dear, perhaps that *would* be best.

JOHN. Look out, he's coming back.

(He raises his revolver as the door opens. Again the CHIEF VILLAIN enters cautiously and creeps towards the window.)

MARY. *(In a whisper)* Shoot!

JOHN. *(Awkwardly)* Er—I suppose it *is* the same man?

MARY. Yes, yes!

JOHN. I mean—it wouldn't be quite fair if— *(He coughs warningly)* Excuse me, sir!

(The CHIEF VILLAIN is now at the window again.)

MARY. Quick, before he goes!

JOHN. *(Raising his revolver nervously)* I ought to

tell you, sir— *(To MARY)* You know, I still think this is a different one.

(The CHIEF VILLAIN again disappears through the window.)

MARY. *(In great disappointment)* Oh, he's gone!

JOHN. *(Firmly)* It was a different one. The other one hadn't got a moustache.

MARY. He had, John. It was the same man, of course it was.

JOHN. Oh! Well, if I had known that, if I had only been certain of it, I should have shot him like a dog.

A VOICE. *(Which sounds like the HERO's)* Help, help!

MARY. John, listen!

JOHN. I *am* listening.

A VOICE. He-e-elp!

MARY. Oughtn't we to do something?

JOHN. We *are* doing something. We're listening. That's what he told us to do.

A VOICE. Help!

JOHN. *(Listening)* That's the other man; the one who came in first.

MARY. The nice-looking one. Oh, John, we *must* do something.

JOHN. If he calls out again, I shall—I shall—do something. I shall take steps. I may even have to shoot somebody. But I will *not* have—

A VOICE. Quick, quick!

MARY. There!

JOHN. Er—was that the same voice?

MARY. *(Moving to the door)* Yes, of course it was. It sounded as if it were in the hall. Come along.

JOHN. Wait a moment. *(She turns round)* We must keep cool, Mary. We mustn't be impetuous. Just hold this a moment. *(He hands her his revolver.)*

MARY. *(Surprised)* Why, what—

JOHN. I shall take my coat off. *(He takes off his coat very slowly)* I'm going through with this. I'm not easily roused, but when once—

A VOICE. Help! Quick!

JOHN. *(Reassuringly)* All right, my man, all right. *(Very leisurely he rolls up his sleeves)* I'm not going to have this sort of thing going on in *my* house. I'm not going to have it. *(Doubtfully)* I don't think I need take my waistcoat off too. What do *you* think, Mary?

MARY. *(Impatiently)* No, dear, of course not, you look very nice.

JOHN. *(Very determined)* Now, then, let's have that revolver. *(She gives it to him)* I shall say "Hands up!" —very sharply, like that—*"Hands up!"*—and then if he doesn't put his hands up I shall—I shall say "Hands up!" again. That will show him that I'm not to be trifled with. Now, then, dear, are you ready?

MARY. *(Eagerly)* Yes!

JOHN. Then—

(But at that moment the LIGHTS go out.)

MARY. Oh!

JOHN. *(Annoyed)* Now, why did you do that, Mary?

MARY. I didn't do it, dear.

JOHN. Then who did?

MARY. I don't know. They just went out.

JOHN. Then I shall write to the company tomorrow and complain. I shall complain to the company about the lights, and I shall complain to the landlord about the way people go in and out of this house, and shriek and—

MARY. *(In alarm)* Oh!

JOHN. *Don't* do that! What is it?

MARY. I can feel somebody quite close to me.

JOHN. Well, that's me.

MARY. Not you, somebody else. . . . Oh! He touched me!

JOHN. *(Addressing the darkness)* Really, sir, I must ask you not to—

MARY. Listen! I can hear breathings all round me!

JOHN. Excuse me, sir, but do you mind *not* breathing all round my wife?

MARY. There! Now I can't hear anything.

JOHN. *(Complacently)* There you are, my dear. You

14

see what firmness does. I wasn't going to have *that* sort of thing going on in my house.

(The LIGHTS go up and reveal the HERO *gagged so that only his eyes are visible, and bound to a chair.)*

MARY. *(Clinging to her husband)* Oh, John!
JOHN. *(With sudden desperate bravery)* Hands up! *(He levels his revolver.)*
MARY. Don't be silly, how can he?
JOHN. All right, dear, I was only practising. *(He blows a speck of dust off his revolver, and holds it up to the light again)* Yes, it's quite a handy little fellow. I think I shall be able to do some business with this all right.
MARY. Poor fellow! I wonder who it is.

(The HERO *tries to speak with his eyes and movements of the head.)*

JOHN. He wants something. Perhaps it's the evening paper. *(He makes a movement towards it.)*
MARY. Listen!

(The HERO *begins to tap with his feet.)*

JOHN. He's signalling something.
MARY. Dots and dashes!
JOHN. That's the Morse Code, that's what that is. Where's my dictionary? *(He fetches it hastily and begins to turn over the pages)*
MARY. Quick, dear!
JOHN. *(Reading)* Here we are. "1. Morse—The walrus." *(Looking at the* HERO*)* No, that must be wrong. Ah, this is better. "2. Morse code signalling of telegraph operators—as 'He sends a good morse.'"
MARY. Well? What does it say?
JOHN. Nothing. That's all. Then we come to "Morsel—a small piece of food, a mouthful, a bite. Also a small meal."

MARY. *(Brilliantly)* A mouthful! That's what he means! He wants the gag taken out of his mouth. *(She goes to him.)*

JOHN. That's very clever of you, Mary. I should never have thought of that.

MARY. *(Untying the gag)* There! . . . Why, it's the man who came in first, the nice-looking one!

JOHN. Yes, he *said* he was coming back.

(Before the HERO *can express his thanks—if that is what he wants to express—the* CHIEF VILLAIN, *accompanied by a* BAD MAN, *comes in.* JOHN *and* MARY *instinctively retreat.)*

CHIEF VILLAIN. *(Sardonically)* Ha!

JOHN. *(Politely)* Ha to you, sir. *(The* CHIEF VILLAIN *fixes* JOHN *with a terrible eye. Nervously to* MARY*)* Say "Ha!" to the gentleman, dear.

MARY. *(Faintly)* Ha!

CHIEF VILLAIN. And what the Mephistopheles are *you* doing here?

JOHN. *(To* MARY*)* What *are* we doing here?

MARY. *(Bravely)* This is our house.

JOHN. Yes, this is *our* house.

CHIEF VILLAIN. Then siddown! *(*JOHN *sits down meekly)* Is this your wife?

JOHN. Yes. *(Making the introduction)* Er—my wife —er—Mr.—er—the gentleman.

CHIEF VILLAIN. Then tell her to siddown too.

JOHN. *(To* MARY*)* He wants you to siddown.

(She does so.)

CHIEF VILLAIN. That's better. *(To* BAD MAN*)* Just take their guns off 'em.

BAD MAN. *(Taking the guns)* Do you want them tied up or gagged or anything?

CHIEF VILLAIN. No, they're not worth it.

JOHN. *(Humbly)* Thank you.

CHIEF VILLAIN. Now, then, to business. *(To* HERO*)* Where's the Rajah's ruby?

16

HERO. *(Firmly)* I shan't tell you.

CHIEF VILLAIN. You won't?

HERO. I won't.

CHIEF VILLAIN. That's awkward. *(After much thought)* You absolutely refuse to?

HERO. I absolutely refuse to.

CHIEF VILLAIN. Ha! *(To* BAD MAN*)* Torture the prisoner.

BAD MAN. *(Cheerfully)* Right you are, governor. *(He feels on the lapel of his coat and then says to* MARY*)* Could you oblige me with the loan of a pin, Mum?

MARY. I don't think— *(Finding one)* Here you are.

BAD MAN. Thanks. *(He advances threateningly upon the prisoner.)*

CHIEF VILLAIN. Wait! *(To* HERO*)* Before proceeding to extremities, I will give you one more chance. Where is the Rujah's Raby?

BAD MAN. You mean the Rabah's Rujy, don't you, governor?

CHIEF VILLAIN. That's what I said.

JOHN. *(Wishing to help)* You *said* the Rubah's Rajy, but I think you meant the rhubarb's—

CHIEF VILLAIN. Silence! *(To* HERO*)* I ask you again —where is the Ruj—I mean where is the Rab— Well, anyhow, where *is* it?

HERO. I won't tell you.

CHIEF VILLAIN. Proceed, Mr. Smithers.

BAD MAN. Well, you've asked for it, Mate. *(He pushes the pin into the* HERO's *arm.)*

HERO. Ow!

MARY. Oh, poor fellow!

CHIEF VILLAIN. Silence! Where is— *(The* HERO *shakes his head)* Torture him again, Mr. Smithers.

HERO. No, no! Mercy! I'll tell you.

JOHN. *(Indignantly)* Oh, I say!

BAD MAN. Shall I just give him another one for luck, governor?

HERO. Certainly not!

JOHN. *(To* MARY*)* Personally I think he should have held out much longer.

17

CHIEF VILLAIN. Very well, then. Where is the Rajah's Ruby?

HERO. In the cloakroom of Waterloo Station. In a hat box.

CHIEF VILLAIN. *(Doubtfully)* In the cloakroom at Waterloo Station, you say?

HERO. Yes. In a hat box. Now release me.

CHIEF VILLAIN. How do I know it's there?

HERO. Well, how do *I* know?

CHIEF VILLAIN. True. *(Holding out his hand)* Well, give me the ticket for it.

HERO. I haven't got it.

BAD MAN. Now, then, none of that.

HERO. I haven't really.

JOHN. I don't think he'd say he *hadn't* got it if he *had* got it. Do you, Mary?

MARY. Oh, I'm sure he wouldn't.

CHIEF VILLAIN. Silence! *(To* HERO*)* Where is the ticket?

HERO. In the cloakroom of Paddington Station. In a hat box.

CHIEF VILLAIN. The same hat box?

HERO. Of course not. The other one was at Waterloo Station.

CHIEF VILLAIN. Well, then, where's the ticket for the hat box in the Paddington cloakroom?

HERO. In the cloakroom at Charing Cross. In a hat box.

CHIEF VILLAIN. *(Annoyed)* Look here, how many hat boxes have you got?

HERO. Lots.

CHIEF VILLAIN. Oh! Now let's get this straight. You say that the Rajah's Ruby is in a hat box in the cloakroom at Paddington—

HERO. Waterloo.

CHIEF VILLAIN. Waterloo; and that the ticket for that hat box is in a hat box in the cloakroom at Euston—

HERO. Paddington.

CHIEF VILLAIN. Paddington; and that the ticket for

this ticket, which is in a hat box at Paddington, for the Ruby which is in a hat box at King's Cross—

BAD MAN. Euston.

JOHN. *(Tentatively)* St. Pancras?

MARY. Earl's Court?

CHIEF VILLAIN. *(Angrily)* Oh, shut up! The ticket for this ticket, which is in a hat box at Paddington, for the Ruby which is in a hat box at—at—

HERO. Waterloo.

CHIEF VILLAIN. Waterloo, thank you. This ticket is in a hat box at—er—

JOHN. *(With decision)* St. Pancras.

MARY. *(Equally certain)* Earl's Court.

CHIEF VILLAIN. *Shut up!* In a hat box at—

HERO. Charing Cross.

CHIEF VILLAIN. Exactly. *(Triumphantly)* Then give me the ticket!

HERO. Which one?

CHIEF VILLAIN. *(Uneasily)* The one we're talking about.

JOHN. *(Helpfully)* The St. Pancras one.

MARY. The Earl's Court one.

CHIEF VILLAIN. *(In a fury) Will* you shut up? *(To* HERO*)* Now listen. *(Very slowly and with an enormous effort of concentration)* I want the ticket for the hat box at Charing Cross, which contains the ticket for the hat box at— (JOHN's *lips indicate "St. Pancras" to* MARY, *whose own seem to express a preference for Earl's Court. The* VILLAIN *gives them one look and goes on firmly)* —at Paddington, which contains the ticket for the hat box at Waterloo, which contains the Rajah's Ruby. *(Proudly)* There!

HERO. I beg your pardon?

CHIEF VILLAIN. *(Violently)* I will *not* say it again! Give me the ticket!

HERO. *(Sadly)* I haven't got it.

CHIEF VILLAIN. *(In an awestruck whisper)* You haven't got it?

HERO. No.

CHIEF VILLAIN. *(After several vain attempts to speak)* Where is it?

HERO. In the cloakroom at Victoria Station.

CHIEF VILLAIN. *(Moistening his lips and speaking faintly)* Not—not in a hat box?

HERO. Yes.

CHIEF VILLAIN. *(Without much hope)* And the ticket for that?

HERO. In the cloakroom at Euston.

CHIEF VILLAIN. *(Quite broken up)* Also in a hat box?

HERO. Yes.

CHIEF VILLAIN. How much longer do we go on?

HERO. *(Cheerfully)* Oh, a long time yet.

CHIEF VILLAIN. *(To* BAD MAN*)* How many London stations are there?

JOHN. Well, there's St. Pancras, and—

MARY. Earl's Court—

BAD MAN. About twenty big ones, governor.

CHIEF VILLAIN. Twenty! *(To* HERO*)* And what do we do when we've gone through the lot?

HERO. Then we go all round them again.

CHIEF VILLAIN. *(Anxiously)* And—and so on?

HERO. And so on.

CHIEF VILLAIN. *(His hand to his head)* This is terrible. I must think. *(To* BAD MAN*)* Just torture him again while I think.

BAD MAN. *(Cheerfully)* Right you are, governor. *(He approaches his victim.)*

HERO. *(Uneasily)* I say, look here!

JOHN. I don't think it's quite fair, you know—

MARY. *(Suddenly)* Give me back my pin!

BAD MAN. Must obey orders, gentlemen. *(Coaxingly to* HERO*)* Just a little way in. *(Indicating with his fingers)* That much.

JOHN. *(To* MARY*)* I think perhaps "that much" wouldn't matter. What do—

CHIEF VILLAIN. *(Triumphantly)* I've got it!

(He rises with an air, the problem solved. They ALL *look at him.)*

JOHN. What?

CHIEF VILLAIN. *(Impressively to* HERO*)* There is somewhere—logically, there must be somewhere—a final, an ultimate hat box.

JOHN. By Jove! That's true!

HERO. Yes.

BAD MAN. *(Scratching his head)* I don't see it.

CHIEF VILLAIN. Then—where *is* that hat box?

JOHN. *(Cheerfully)* St. Pancras.

MARY. Earl's Court.

CHIEF VILLAIN. Shut up! *(To* HERO*)* Where is that hat box?

HERO. In the cloakroom at Charing Cross.

CHIEF VILLAIN. Ah! *(He holds out his hand)* Then give me the ticket for it.

BAD MAN. *(Threateningly)* Come on now! The ticket!

HERO. *(Shaking his head sadly)* I can't.

CHIEF VILLAIN. *(Almost inarticulate with emotion)* You don't mean to say you've—lost—it?

HERO. *(In a whisper, with bowed head)* I've lost it.

(With a terrible shriek the CHIEF VILLAIN *falls back fainting into the arms of the* BAD MAN. *Instinctively* JOHN *and* MARY *embrace, sobbing to each other, "He's lost it!" The* HEROINE *rushes in, crying, "My love, you've lost it!" and puts her arms round the* HERO. *Only the* MAN IN THE BOWLER HAT *remains unmoved. Slowly he removes the cigar from his mouth and speaks.)*

BOWLER HAT. Yes. . . . That's all right. . . . Just a bit ragged still. . . . We'll take it again at eleven to-morrow . . . Second Act, please.

(And so the rehearsal goes on.)

OTHER TITLES AVAILABLE FROM SAMUEL FRENCH

TREASURE ISLAND
Ken Ludwig

All Groups / Adventure / 10m, 1f (doubling) / Areas
Based on the masterful adventure novel by Robert Louis Stevenson, *Treasure Island* is a stunning yarn of piracy on the tropical seas. It begins at an inn on the Devon coast of England in 1775 and quickly becomes an unforgettable tale of treachery and mayhem featuring a host of legendary swashbucklers including the dangerous Billy Bones (played unforgettably in the movies by Lionel Barrymore), the sinister two-timing Israel Hands, the brassy woman pirate Anne Bonney, and the hideous form of evil incarnate, Blind Pew. At the center of it all are Jim Hawkins, a 14-year-old boy who longs for adventure, and the infamous Long John Silver, who is a complex study of good and evil, perhaps the most famous hero-villain of all time. Silver is an unscrupulous buccaneer-rogue whose greedy quest for gold, coupled with his affection for Jim, cannot help but win the heart of every soul who has ever longed for romance, treasure and adventure.

OTHER TITLES AVAILABLE FROM SAMUEL FRENCH

TAKE HER, SHE'S MINE
Phoebe and Henry Ephron

Comedy / 11m, 6f / Various Sets

Art Carney and Phyllis Thaxter played the Broadway roles of parents of two typical American girls enroute to college. The story is based on the wild and wooly experiences the authors had with their daughters, Nora Ephron and Delia Ephron, themselves now well known writers. The phases of a girl's life are cause for enjoyment except to fearful fathers. Through the first two years, the authors tell us, college girls are frightfully sophisticated about all departments of human life. Then they pass into the "liberal" period of causes and humanitarianism, and some into the intellectual lethargy of beatniksville. Finally, they start to think seriously of their lives as grown ups. It's an experience in growing up, as much for the parents as for the girls.

"A warming comedy. A delightful play about parents vs kids. It's loaded with laughs. It's going to be a smash hit."
– *New York Mirror*